To my mother and my late father with my heartfelt appreciation for the wonderful childhood memories they provided me.　　– SB

To all of the children in both Japan and the U.S. who have shown me the true meaning of cross-cultural understanding.　　– WM

Published by Tuttle Publishing, an imprint of Periplus Editions (HK) Ltd.

www.tuttlepublishing.com

Copyright © 2010 by Setsu Broderick

Library of Congress Cataloging-in-Publication Data

Broderick, Setsu.
Japanese traditions : rice cakes, cherry blossoms, and matsuri : a year of seasonal Japanese festivities / text by Setsu Broderick & Willamarie Moore ; illustrations by Setsu Broderick.
 48 p. : col. ill. ; 24 x 28 cm.
 ISBN 978-4-8053-1089-2 (hd. cover)
1. Festivals--Japan. 2. Japan--Social life and customs. 3. Rites and ceremonies--Japan. I. Moore, Willamarie. II. Title.
 GT4884.A2B76 2010
 394.26952--dc22
　　　　　2009032927

ISBN: 978-4-8053-1089-2
ISBN: 978-4-8053-1909-3 (for sale in Japan only)

Distributed by

North America, Latin America & Europe
Tuttle Publishing
364 Innovation Drive
North Clarendon, VT 05759-9436 U.S.A.
Tel: 1 (802) 773-8930; Fax: 1 (802) 773-6993
info@tuttlepublishing.com; www.tuttlepublishing.com

Japan
Tuttle Publishing
Yaekari Building, 3rd Floor
5-4-12 Osaki, Shinagawa-ku, Tokyo 141 0032
Tel: (81) 3 5437-0171; Fax: (81) 3 5437-0755
sales@tuttle.co.jp; www.tuttle.co.jp

Asia Pacific
Berkeley Books Pte. Ltd.
3 Kallang Sector #04-01, Singapore 349278
Tel: (65) 6741-2178; Fax: (65) 6741-2179
inquiries@periplus.com.sg; www.tuttlepublishing.com

First edition
27 26 25 24　　11 10 9 8　　2405CM
Printed in China

TUTTLE PUBLISHING® is a registered trademark of Tuttle Publishing, a division of Periplus Editions (HK) Ltd.

"Books to Span the East and West"

Tuttle Publishing was founded in 1832 in the small New England town of Rutland, Vermont [USA]. Our core values remain as strong today as they were then—to publish best-in-class books which bring people together one page at a time. In 1948, we established a publishing outpost in Japan—and Tuttle is now a leader in publishing English-language books about the arts, languages and cultures of Asia. The world has become a much smaller place today and Asia's economic and cultural influence has grown. Yet the need for meaningful dialogue and information about this diverse region has never been greater. Over the past seven decades, Tuttle has published thousands of books on subjects ranging from martial arts and paper crafts to language learning and literature—and our talented authors, illustrators, designers and photographers have won many prestigious awards. We welcome you to explore the wealth of information available on Asia at **www.tuttlepublishing.com**.

Japanese Traditions

Rice Cakes, Cherry Blossoms and Matsuri
A Year of Seasonal Japanese Festivities

Illustrations by Setsu Broderick

Text by Setsu Broderick and Willamarie Moore

TUTTLE Publishing

Tokyo | Rutland, Vermont | Singapore

This book is a look back at when I was growing up in the Japanese countryside about 50 years ago. I invite you to visit my beautiful country village with me and share some of the happy times of my childhood through these words and paintings.

Each of the large paintings represents a month of the year. Look carefully at each painting, there's a lot to see. There will probably be a few things that you won't recognize and might wonder about. For that reason, my friend Willamarie and I have included some additional information on the pages that follow each month. Also, at the end of the book, we've included an activity called *Let's Look More Closely!* for you to find and think about what's happening in the paintings.

Psst, I'll tell you my secret. I used to be one of them, a little country kitten. "MEOW!"

— *Setsu*

January

Happy New Year! Akemashite omedetō!
There was nothing as joyful in our childhood as New Year's Day, and we could hardly wait for it to come. On New Year's Day, families and friends enjoyed delicious New Year's food and had fun together all day long. Outside, we flew kites, spun colorful tops, and played *hanetsuki* (a game like badminton). Inside, we played *sugoroku* (similar to backgammon) and card games like *karuta*.

One evening in the middle of January, our village celebrated the Tondo Festival. The men built a tall tower with bundles of bamboo. Then everyone brought their used New Year's decorations and the whole thing was lit on fire. People prayed for their family's happiness and good health through the year. It was very exciting to see the big flames and sparks lighting up the dark sky.

We toasted *kagami-mochi* (large rice cakes) on the fire embers, and everyone ate them for good luck in the coming year. Somehow, the rice cakes always turned out to be charred … but we didn't mind eating them anyway!

Tondo Festival

4

New Year Traditions

Kakizome (Calligraphy)

Traditionally, on January 2nd, children write special New Year's calligraphy. The words they choose symbolize their wishes or resolutions for the New Year. For example, two of the words written here are: *shinsetsu* ("kindness") and *tomodachi* ("friend").

Daruma Doll

Daruma is said to have brought Zen Buddhism to Japan. Legend tells that he sat in a cave meditating for so long that he lost the use of his arms and legs! This is why *Daruma* dolls are round, and if you try to knock them over, they go upright again. *Daruma* represents determination. Often, people get a *Daruma* doll when they want to achieve some goal. They write their goal on the back, color in one eye, and then do everything they can to achieve that goal. When they do, they color in the second eye to celebrate their success!

Nenga-jo (New Year's Cards) >

People send *nenga-jo*, postcards with New Year Greetings, to family and friends. Usually, they write standard phrases and a few sentences about what they did in the past year, or their New Year resolutions. It's also common to decorate the card with the Zodiac animal of the year. For example, 2010 is the Year of the Tiger.

Usually, the postman brings a big delivery of all the postcards sent to each family from their friends and relatives from all over the country. It's fun to read them all together!

New Year Games

Hanetsuki & Koma

In *hanetsuki*, which is similar to badminton, two players hit a birdie back and forth with a decorated wooden paddle called *hagoita*. The one who lets it drop to the ground gets a black ink mark on her face!

Koma, or spinning tops, is fun to play. The tops are spun either by hand or with a string. In one game each player spins their top within a circle and tries to knock the other top out of bounds.

< Tako-age (Kite-flying)

Japanese kites are made of paper glued onto a thin bamboo frame. They come in many different shapes and sizes, and are decorated with faces of samurai or kabuki actors, or with calligraphy.

Fukuwarai >

In this game, one person is blindfolded, and then tries to put all of the parts (mouth, nose, eyes, eyebrows) onto a blank face. It's fun to see the comical results!

February

February was the coldest month and we had many snowy days.

Our school was very old and the classrooms were drafty and cold in the winter. We warmed our hands at the big charcoal brazier in the classroom but, as soon as it was time for recess, we rushed outside for snowball fights. When we came home after school, we crawled under the *kotatsu*, a heated table with a quilt to cover your lap. At the *kotatsu* we did homework, read books, played games, and took naps. Also, the whole family sat together and ate meals there. In those days, the *kotatsu* and charcoal brazier were the only sources of heat in the house.

At bedtime, my mother put hot water bottles in everyone's beds to keep us warm through the night. The coldest thing, though, was the portable water sprinkling can for washing hands that hung outside of the bathroom window. There was nothing as cold as this water, especially on a snowy day! Still, we always wished for a lot of snow to make a big snowman or a snow rabbit.

Winter Fun

Setsubun

In early February, *Setsubun* celebrates the coming of spring. People traditionally believe that evil spirits emerge when the seasons turn. So on this day, people open the doors of their houses and throw roasted soybeans out (or at a family member wearing an ogre's mask) and shout, "Demons out! Fortune in!" This is said to help purify the home by driving away the evil spirits and bad health. Then, to welcome in health and good fortune, everyone eats the same number of soybeans as their age.

< Jan-Ken-Pon Game (Rock-Scissors-Paper)

Ken means "fist" in Japanese, and this is a game using only your hands. Two or more people can play. You say, "Jan-Ken…" and on "Pon!" everyone puts their hand into the circle with one of three gestures: a fist means rock, two fingers out means scissors, and a flat palm means paper. Rock beats scissors; scissors beats paper; and paper beats rock. Sometimes you have to go for many rounds before a winner emerges! It's a fun game, and also a common way for a group of people to make quick decisions.

Staying Warm

Kotatsu (Low Heated Table)

A *kotatsu* is a square table with a heater underneath. In the old days, it was a charcoal heater; nowadays, the heater is electric and plugs in. You place a quilt-like cover between the tabletop and frame, and you sit with the quilt over your lap to keep warm. Of course, children and pets like to crawl underneath and use the quilt to cover their whole body!

Charcoal Brazier at School
In the old days, this was the only source of heat in the classroom. In between lessons, kids would gather around to get warm.

Soroban (Abacus)
This is a traditional calculator, used for counting and doing math problems. Even today, children in Japan learn how to use the abacus.

March

Spring at last!

Sometimes we had a dusting of snow in early March, but mostly there were signs of spring everywhere in the village. The grass began to grow in the fields and we enjoyed gathering the new sprouts of herbs and edible wild plants. My mother would cook our favorite spring dishes when we brought home a basketful of fresh sprouts.

March 3rd was *Hina Matsuri*, the Doll Festival, also called Girls' Day. On this day, girls were celebrated with a set of beautiful Japanese dolls and delicious treats to wish for their future happiness and good health. And we girls spent the day playing with dolls, *origami*, Japanese beanbags, marbles, and playing house.

In late March at school, there was graduation and the term closing ceremony. Then Spring Break started. During Spring Break, it became warmer day by day and we played in the flowery green fields from morning until dusk. March was also the beautiful time of plum and peach blossoms in the village.

Hina Matsuri (Doll Festival or Girls' Day)

March 3rd is a day devoted to girls. On this occasion, a family wishes for their daughters' health and happiness. Often girls dress up in silk *kimono* and visit each other's homes to admire their doll displays. They enjoy eating *ocha-gashi* (small tea cakes) and *sekihan* (rice cooked with red azuki beans), and drinking *amazake* (a sweet drink made from rice).

Origami (Paper Folding) ∧

The art of folding paper to create beautiful objects dates back many centuries in Japan. All kids learn basic *origami* either at home or at school. The most common *origami* figure is the crane. Cranes are a symbol of long life. If someone is sick, friends and family may fold 1,000 paper cranes and string them together as a way to wish for their recovery.

< Hina Dolls

A special set of dolls dressed in traditional costumes is displayed on tiered shelves. But the dolls are not for playing with! They are ceremonial dolls that represent the ancient imperial court, and are meant to be looked at and admired. The dolls are usually put away by mid-March. Some people believe their daughters will have a hard time marrying if the dolls are kept out too long.

Japanese Food

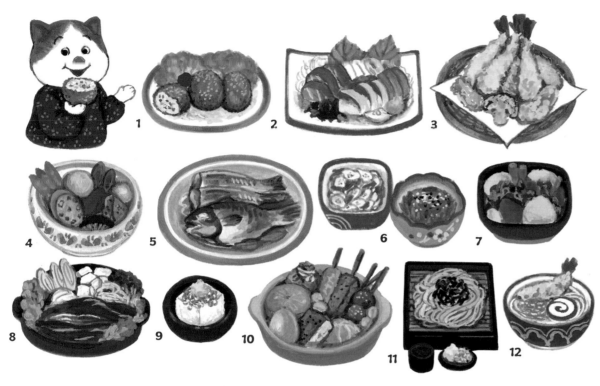

Gohan literally means "steamed rice," but is also the word for "food" in Japan. Most meals consist of rice, a main dish of fish or meat, vegetables, soup, and pickles. Because Japan is surrounded by oceans, fish and seafood dishes are very common. Soup is drunk straight from the bowl (no spoons necessary!). And the rice is very sticky, so is easy to eat with chopsticks.

Names of foods:
1. *Korokke* (meat and potato croquette)
2. *Sashimi* (raw fish)
3. *Tempura* (deep-fried seafood & vegetables)
4. *Nishime* (cooked vegetables)
5. *Nizakana* (cooked fish)
6. *Aemono* (salad)
7. *Nikujaga* (cooked meat & vegetables)
8. *Sukiyaki* (sliced meat & vegetables)
9. *Tofu* (bean curd)
10. *Oden* (seafood & vegetables in broth)
11. *Soba* (buckwheat noodles)
12. *Udon* (wheat-flour noodles)

Rice Bowl and Chopsticks
Usually, each person gets their own bowl of rice, bowl of soup, and small plate of pickles. The main dish and other side dishes are in serving dishes in the middle of the table.

Rice Cakes
There are many different snacks and sweets made with rice. Those shown on the left are salty, crunchy snacks called *senbei* or *arare*. On the right are *mochi* and *o-hagi*. They are sweet and chewy, and usually eaten with green tea.

Chirashi-zushi
This is a colorful rice dish with many different kinds of fish, vegetables, and egg scattered within. It is commonly eaten on Girls' Day.

April

It was as if we were living on a planet of flowers!
The hills, the fields, the whole village was covered with flowers of pink, red, white, yellow, purple and blue.

Early April was the season for cherry (*sakura*) blossoms in our village, and there was a day for *o-hanami*, the Cherry Blossom Viewing Festival. On that day, we children got together and headed to the round mountain of *sakura* trees, our backpacks full with our special picnic lunch. We walked through the field, across the log bridge and up the slope to the mountaintop. By the time we got there, we were so hungry that we eagerly enjoyed the festive lunch. We spent many hours there playing hide and seek, climbing trees like Tarzan, and playing tag. We enjoyed playing and eating so much that we often forgot about admiring the beautiful *sakura* blossoms!

Soon afterwards, the new school year started. The annual school photo was taken with our new classmates under the *sakura* tree in the schoolyard.

四月

Cherry Blossom Season

While many kinds of flowers blossom in Japan, people's favorite flower is *sakura*, the cherry blossom, and April is the time for *sakura*. The color and shape of the flowers symbolize purity and simplicity, and their short-lived bloom reflects the shortness of life. Even the slightest breeze causes the petals to shower down like pink snow.

Bento (Boxed Lunch) ∨
A picnic lunch is packed in a box, called a *bento*. Typically, each *bento* is a balanced meal, compact, and pretty to look at. Half of the box is filled with rice—often with *umeboshi* (pickled plum) in the middle—and the other half has several side dishes.

O-hanami (Flower-viewing) ∧
People celebrate with family, friends and co-workers by holding picnics under the trees in full bloom. This tradition dates back to ancient times, when people wrote poetry and sang songs inspired by the flowering trees.

Off to School >
In Japan, the new school year starts in April. Many schools require students to wear uniforms, sometimes with a cap. There is also a standard backpack that is traditionally red for girls and black for boys.

Japanese Houses

Greeting Visitors at the Genkan

In Japan, people take off their shoes when entering a home. The area where you remove (and put on) your shoes is called the *genkan*. From there, you step up into the house. It's polite to say "*Ojama-shimasu*," which means, "Excuse me for disturbing you," when you first arrive. And people often bring a small gift, called an *omiyage*.

Maneki-neko (Beckoning Cat)

You often see *maneki-neko* at the entrances of shops and houses. Some people think it brings prosperity. One paw is up, scratching its ear and waving in customers or visitors. The other paw often holds an old coin, meant to attract money.

Bonsai

Bonsai are miniature trees grown in containers. It takes very special skill and technique to grow, shape, and care for *bonsai*. But when done well, they can live for hundreds of years!

Tatami

The floors of traditional Japanese rooms are covered with rectangular *tatami* mats made of rice straw and woven rush. In *tatami* rooms, people usually sit on the floors or on pillows called *zabutons*.

19

May

Huge, colorful carp streamers flew in the blue May sky: Boys' Festival!

In May, the bamboo shoots sprung up here and there and everywhere in the bamboo grove. It was fun to go bamboo shoot picking. The young bamboo shoots, wrapped in their husks, were very tender. So it was easy for us to break them—snap, snap, snap!—and we would bring a bundle of shoots home. My mother looked at the bundle, picked one of them, and said, "This is the best one. I'll cook a delicious dinner tonight." We used the rest of the shoots to make toys and play with.

One of the busiest times of the year for farmers was rice planting. Farmers worked all day long in their fields. Sometimes, when they sat on the grass to rest, the peddler showed up. He opened his big pack, pulled out a lot of different things, and spread them out on a large cloth, making a miniature market. It was amazing— he had everything from daily goods to clothes, fish and meat, and even… "Our favorite candies!" we would exclaim with delight. We thought he was as great as a magician.

五月

Kodomo no Hi *(Boys' Festival or Children's Day)*

May 5th is Boys' Festival (now called Children's Day). Traditionally, families with boys displayed samurai dolls or suits of armor in their homes and flew carp-shaped streamers outdoors. It was a time to pray for their sons to grow up to be healthy and brave. Nowadays people honor both boys and girls on this day.

One tradition of the holiday involves iris leaves. The leaves are used to decorate roofs—in order to keep evil spirits and diseases away. In addition, the leaves are put into the hot bath. This was meant to strengthen people for the heat and hard work of the upcoming summer.

Samurai Armor
Samurai were Japanese warriors active between the 12th and 19th centuries. They carried out their duties with a variety of weapons but were most famous for their use of the sword. Samurai lived their lives according to a strict code of behavior, including loyalty, self-discipline, and respect—qualities that are still important in Japan today.

Origami Helmet
Here's how you can make a samurai helmet.

Made with 7-inch square paper, this hat will fit a child's beanbag toy. To make a full-size hat for a child, begin with a 20-inch square of paper. For an adult, use 22-inch paper.

1. Fold horizontally as shown from top to bottom.

2. Valley-fold left point B down to meet point A. Valley-fold right point D down to meet point A.

3. Fold points B and D up so that they meet at point E.

4. Fold point B along dotted line MO. Fold point D along the dotted line NO.

5. Your paper should look like this. Valley-fold point A along dotted line XY.

6. Valley-fold edge XY so that it meets at FG.

7. Your paper will look like this. Turn the paper over.

8. Fold C all the way up to meet point E. Turn the paper over.

9. The finished helmet.

Mochi
Everyone enjoys eating *kashiwa-mochi*, sticky rice cakes with sweet beans inside and wrapped in oak leaves.

Toys and Games

Sumo (Wrestling)

In the sport in *sumo*, two wrestlers battle each other in a ring. You win by knocking the other person out of the ring or down to the ground. Professional sumo wrestlers train from a young age, and eat a special diet that puts on as much weight as possible, while also building muscles.

Kamifusen (Paper Balloon)

This balloon is made from colorful Japanese paper. You blow it up through the hole at one end and then toss it or hit it in the air. It's also fun to try balancing on a finger or your head!

Taketonbo (Bamboo Dragonfly)

Twist these bamboo toys really fast between your hands and watch them fly off like a dragonfly!

Kendama (Ball and Stick Game)

Toss the ball and try to catch it in one of the cups or spear it with the point at the top. There are many different techniques—it's harder than it looks!

June

Rain, rain, go away!

The rainy season, known as *tsuyu* in Japan, begins in June and usually lasts for the month. It would rain off-and-on almost every day, sometimes lightly, sometimes in a downpour. Sometimes the rain was so heavy that the floodwaters carried away the wooden bridges and some children could not go to school. But whenever we saw the sunlight between rainy periods, we ran outside happily and played as long as we could. The rest of the time, we had fun indoors.

In those days, before TV or computers, one of our favorite pastimes was listening to the daily radio drama, especially the series of exciting *ninja* stories. It was broadcast around 5 o'clock every day. Kids would rush home, gather 'round the radio, and sing along with the theme song. It was fun to talk with classmates at school about the previous day's episode and try to guess what was going to happen on the next show.

When walking in the rain, we used umbrellas made of oiled-paper, called *karakasa*. They looked so pretty and made a tap-tap, pitter-patter sound when it rained. I loved that sound—it was like the rain singing.

When we came home from school, we would go to a nearby rice-paddy to play with the frogs and tadpoles. It was so much fun playing in the mud! We would get all covered with mud and make a mess of some of the rice plants. Almost every day we had to say, "We're sorry, we won't do it again!"

六月

Rainy Season

Teru-teru Bozu (Fine-weather Dolls)

Teru means "to shine" and *bozu* means "Buddhist priest" (or is slang for "bald-headed"). *Teru-teru bozu* are dolls made of white paper or cloth and hung up with strings in front of the windows. Children make *teru-teru bozu* during the rainy season or before a picnic or sports day to wish for good weather.

Karakasa
This traditional, handmade umbrella has a bamboo frame and is covered with paper that is oiled to make it waterproof.

Geta
These traditional sandals make a loud "clack-clack" sound when you walk. They keep your feet high off the ground so they stay dry in the rain.

Growing Rice
Depending on the region, rice is planted between late April and June. Traditionally, each rice seedling was planted by hand, one by one in neat rows, so it took a lot of time and effort. People often worked from dawn to dusk, and everyone helped out. The rice plants must remain in water to grow strong, so that's why the fields are so wet and muddy at this time of year!

26

Indoor Fun

Radio Drama

Kids used to rush home to listen to the daily radio show about *ninja*.

Ninja

Disguised all in black, *ninja* were special spies in old Japan. Their job was to discover enemy secrets, destroy their weapons, and kill their leaders. They knew how to move around without making a single sound, climb walls and travel across rooftops, go underwater, and use visual tricks to disappear in an instant.

Fusuma and Shoji

These two types of sliding panels can act as doors, walls, and sometimes even windows! Thin *shoji* paper allows light to filter through. *Fusuma* may be painted, as they are here. *Fusuma* between rooms can be removed to create a larger room.

Kamishibai (Paper Drama)

This form of storytelling dates back almost 1,000 years! A *kamishibai* storyteller would ride by bicycle from town to town and set up his storytelling box in a park. He announced his arrival with a pair of wooden clappers and people would gather to hear the stories. Children who bought candy would get the best seats. The storyteller told his stories using a set of illustrated boards, inserted into the box and taken out one by one as the story was told. Many stories were serials and new episodes were told on each visit. Often, children made their own *kamishibai* stages out of cardboard, and told traditional folk stories, like *Momotaro*, the Peach Boy, as shown here.

July

Our village in July was filled with the sounds of summer.

There were the loud chorus of frogs in the rice fields, the never-ending buzzing of cicadas in the trees, and the deep rumblings of big thunderstorms. Our favorite, of course, was the "ring-ring-ring" bells of the ice-candy man. And the beautiful sounds of the tinkling of the wind chimes in the evening.

In those days, our neighbors—both adults and children—got together on summer nights and enjoyed chatting or playing Japanese chess (*Shogi*) on the veranda. That was always a wonderful time and one of my happiest memories of summertime.

We didn't have screen windows, but we had room-sized mosquito nets to sleep under. "Yoo-hoo! Come and see the fireflies! They are all over the yard!" Sometimes fireflies flew into the house through open windows. When we were lying under the mosquito net and there were many fireflies flying in the dark room, it seemed as if we were sleeping under the stars. And then, someone would always exclaim, "Ah, a mosquito! A mosquito is inside!"

七月

Tanabata Matsuri (Star Festival)

Tanabata Matsuri, the Star Festival, is celebrated on the seventh day of the seventh month. *Tanabata* commemorates the meeting of two lovers who lived on opposite sides of the Milky Way. They were allowed to meet only once a year on this night.

To celebrate the festival, people write wishes—sometimes as poems—on strips of colorful paper and then hang them with other small decorations on bamboo branches set up in front of the house.

Catching Bugs ∧

Many Japanese children love to collect bugs and keep them in cages. Sometimes they observe them for summer homework projects.

Here, two kittens are trying to catch a cicada. Cicadas live in the trees and sing loud buzzing songs in the summer. The most popular bugs to catch are beetles, because they can grow to nearly three inches in length, and they bear impressive "horns" that look like samurai helmet ornaments.

Staying Cool

Summertime gets very hot and humid in Japan, so people have many different ways to stay cool.

Sudare (Shades)
Special bamboo or reed shades, called *sudare*, are hung on verandas and outside shops to keep the hot sun and insects out, while allowing the cool breeze in. They are usually put up in the spring and taken down in the fall.

Bamboo Water Pistol
Children used to make a type of water gun out of bamboo. It was fun to play outside on a hot day, shooting water at each other!

Fans
There are many types of fans in Japan. Handheld fans are most often made of paper on a bamboo frame, usually with a design painted on them. Some fans, called *sensu*, fold up to a compact size easy for carrying; others, called *uchiwa*, are flat.

Kakigōri (Shaved Ice)
Shaved ice flavored with syrup is always a favorite summertime treat. It comes in lots of tasty flavors, such as green tea, lemon, and strawberry!

August

August was the most fun month of the year: summer vacation!

The only thing that was not-so-fun was *Rajio Taisō*, the daily morning exercise program at 6:30 a.m.! But after that we played all day long. We loved playing in the river, swimming, fishing, scooping up minnows, and collecting pretty pebbles. At home, we would fall asleep on the veranda for a heavenly afternoon nap, and would awaken to a delicious snack of chilled watermelon. We liked to have watermelon seed-spitting contests, too. At night, we played with fireworks, created our own shadow plays, and told each other spooky ghost stories.

The biggest event of summer was the *Bon* Festival in mid-August. People welcomed their ancestors' spirits and visited their families' graves to pray and offer food and flowers.

There was only one problem we had during summer vacation: homework! We had a lot of it, and we had to finish by the end of August. Of course, I always waited until the last two days of vacation… and had to work sooo hard to finish it all at the last minute with my mother's help. Then I was told sternly how I should spend my vacation next year…

八月

O-Bon Festival (Festival of the Souls)

O-Bon is the most important Buddhist festival in Japan. People return to their hometowns and gather with their extended families. They welcome their ancestors' spirits back for this time by visiting their grave sites, praying at the family altar, and lighting lanterns and small fires in front of their homes. In the village center, a big festival site is set up: a tall stage tower is erected for musicians and colorful lanterns are hung all around. Vendors set up stalls to sell food and drink and toys and games.

Taiko (Drum)
Taiko are one of the most important instruments at Japanese festivals. They come in many sizes. The huge ones are so big they are struck from the side, and take the drummer's full body effort to play!

Bon Dance
People gather around the stage and do a special dance called *bon odori* all evening. Everyone joins in—old and young, big and small—dancing in a circle 'round the tower.

Yukata
People often dress in *yukata* for summer festivals. *Yukata* are made of lightweight cotton and are easier to move around in, compared to the more formal *kimono*. Especially on a hot August night, *yukata* are best!

Summer Fun

O-bake (Ghosts) ∧
O-bake are supernatural beings that have temporarily changed into another form. Their true form is often an animal such as a fox or badger. *Yūrei* are the ghosts of people. They usually appear between 2 and 3 a.m. to haunt those who caused them harm. You can usually tell one by its white clothing, long, messed-up hair, and missing legs or feet.

Rajio Taisō (Radio Calisthenics)

"Arms up – 2 – 3! To the side – 2 – 3! Bend forward – 2 – 3! Arch back – 2 – 3!"

Daily warm-up exercises known as *Rajio Taisō* have been popular in Japan for almost 100 years. In the old days during summer vacation, students were required to participate in *Rajio Taisō* as part of their summer homework. They had to show up every morning at 6:30 a.m. and follow along. Each day, the kids had to get their attendance card stamped and then turn it in at the end of the summer with the rest of their homework.

These days kids do such exercises at school (in gym class or at assemblies) and adults do them at the office (in the morning or after lunch). The idea is not only to promote health, but also group unity and cooperation—important aspects of Japanese culture.

September

Heating the bath

September was a month for beautiful red dragonflies, lovely cosmos flowers blossoming everywhere, and the singing of autumn insects.

On the night of the full moon, we had *tsukimi*, the harvest moon-viewing party. The harvest moon was one of the most beautiful of the year, with its perfectly round shape and spectacular bright light.

At the end of September, it started to become cool, especially at night. When we came home from playing outside in the early evening, our favorite thing to do was to watch the burning twigs in the furnace that heated the water for the bath. Then, while soaking in the warm bath, we enjoyed looking at the beautiful red sunset through the window, until the first star of the evening twinkled.

36

九月

Enjoying Nature

Tsukimi (Moon-Viewing) >

Traditionally, on the evening of the full moon, people decorated the veranda with Japanese pampas grass and other autumn flowers, and set out a tray of offerings of rice wine and sweet dumplings. Then they enjoyed the beautiful full moon together. Sometimes they wrote poetry. Sometimes they told folk stories.

One story is that there was a rabbit in the moon pounding *mochi* (sticky rice) with a big mortar and pestle. To this day, people in Japan see the rabbit in the moon (like elsewhere, people see a man in the moon).

< O-furo (Japanese Bath)

In Japan, the daily bath is usually taken at night. The idea is not only to clean yourself, but also to relax and rid yourself of the day's worries. As there is usually only one bath in each house, everyone in the family takes turns. Kids often bathe together. The water in the tub is heated very hot, and the tub is covered to keep it hot. First, in the shower area outside of the tub, you use soap to get yourself squeaky clean. Only then do you enter the tub. This is important, since everyone uses the same bathwater!

38

Harvest Time

< Harvest Festival

In the autumn, in rural villages across Japan, people celebrate the successful rice harvest. To give thanks for another bountiful year, the first crops to be harvested are offered to the gods. Then everyone has fun at the festival site. Food stalls sell grilled octopus balls, grilled squid, cotton candy, and other festival foods. Other booths sell all kinds of toys and games. Everyone comes out to enjoy the day.

Shishimai (Lion Dance) >

The Lion Dance originally came to Japan from China. It is performed at different times of the year, often at harvest festivals. Usually two men wear a costume and a big, scary lion head with a mouth that moves. The lion dances to music played on bamboo flutes and drums. For the harvest festival, the lion comes to dance at every household to ward off evil spirits and ensure a good harvest. It is said that if the lion nips the head of a child, she/he will be protected. But for little children, it's very scary!

October

Mikoshi being carried to the village shrine

When the rice fields turned a shining golden color, it was time for the harvest.
The farmers of the village got busy harvesting the rice from their fields. Children got busy gathering chestnuts and picking persimmons from the trees… and sometimes had fun tossing the persimmons at each other!

The most fun October day for us was the Autumn Festival, held to celebrate and give thanks for the autumn harvest. The day before the festival, *Shishimai*, the lion dance, was performed at every house to drive evil spirits out. The day of the festival, the newly harvested rice was offered to the gods and a large group of men carried the *mikoshi* (portable shrine) as they marched to the village shrine. There were a lot fair booths, which were very crowded with people all day long. At the booths, there was anything and everything that children wanted, like dolls, colorful balloons, tin model cars, coloring books, monster masks, marbles, big cotton candies and more. We were so excited that it made us feel as if we were in Toyland!

十月

November

Autumn Leaves

It became colder by the day. At the beginning of November, the mountains put on autumn colors and the beautiful foliage season arrived in the village. The trees and shrubs of our neighborhood turned deep red and bright gold. But, as soon as the wintry cold blast hit the trees, the leaves were blown off and the gardens and the sidewalks were covered with colorful fallen leaves. We enjoyed crunching through the thick blanket of leaves as we started our daily chore: to rake the fallen leaves into piles. We loved to make a great big pile of leaves and jump into it. As we came out, we were covered with leaves, and everyone looked like leaf monsters.

Our favorite thing was to make an open fire with the pile of fallen leaves. We huddled around the warmth and sometimes we tucked sweet potatoes in the fire to bake. Then we would forget about them until someone called, "Come on, guys! Sweet potatoes are ready!" And we discovered the forgotten sweet potatoes had become charcoal!

42

十一月

Getting Colder

Sleeping on Futon >

Traditionally in Japan, you sleep on the floor. The bed is called a *futon*, and is taken out of the closet at bedtime. First, you spread out the *shiki-buton*, the mattress, on the bottom, and then you cover yourself with the *kake-buton*, the thick quilt comforter. Pillows are traditionally filled with buckwheat husks, and bend to the shape of your head. In the morning, you fold up the futon and put it back in the closet.

< Inoko Matsuri

In early November, *Inoko Matsuri* takes place to celebrate children's good health and prosperity, and to pray for the future generations to come.

On this day, children carry a decorated small *Inoko* stone around to every house in the neighborhood. The stone has enough ropes for each child to hold onto. Then together, they pound the ground, sing the *Inoko* song, and men in scary ogre masks come to drive away the evil spirits. At night everyone enjoys special foods for the occasion.

44

Visiting the Shrine

O-mamori (Good Luck Charm) ∧
Mamori means "protection." Whenever you go to a shrine or temple, you can buy a little amulet called *o-mamori* to bring you luck or protection. For example, there are *o-mamori* for good health; to protect you while traveling; to wish for love and marriage; or for success in school! Inside the cloth wrapping, there are pieces of paper or wood with prayers written on them. But you are never supposed to open it—you just keep it with you or in a special place.

Shichi-Go-San (7-5-3 Festival) ∧
On November 15th, boys and girls who are three years old, boys who are five, and girls who are seven all dress up in beautiful traditional clothing (*kimono* for girls, *haori* jackets and *hakama* pants for boys), and go to the local shrine. The priests bless them for good health. Then they receive special sweets called *chitose-ame*, or "long life candy." The candy is shaped in long sticks and comes in bags decorated with cranes and turtles, animals that symbolize long life.

December

Busy... busy... busy...

December was a very busy month for everyone. There were so many things to do at the end of the year, and we cherished the old customs and events. One custom is to do a general year-end cleaning both inside and outside of the house. Our house cleaning started in the early morning and continued into the evening, dusting, sweeping, polishing and repapering the *shoji* doors. Then we decorated the house with New Year's ornaments—that was my grandpa's job. My grandma was busy making the vegetable pickles in a large barrel—it was her specialty.

Another big event was the rice cake making: hot steamed rice was poured into a giant mortar and was pounded with a pestle until it got really sticky. Then we shaped it into large round rice cakes. These rice cakes were offered to the gods on New Year's Day.

On New Year's Eve, my mother cooked all day to make the special foods for the holidays. That night, everyone ate *toshi-koshi soba* (buckwheat noodles) and waited to hear the bells from the temple at midnight. I was never able to stay up that late and just fell asleep. But surely I was dreaming of a wonderful New Year's Day.

十二月

Getting Ready for New Year

Shimekazari (Wreath)
Made of rice straw and a *"dai dai"* (a Japanese bitter orange), *shimekazari* are hung over the front door to keep evil spirits away.

Kadomatsu (Gate pine)
These special decorations are made from three stalks of bamboo, cut diagonally at different heights. They are bound together with straw, and then pine branches are added. Bamboo represents strength and resilience; pine represents constancy and long life. *Kadomatsu* usually come in pairs, and are set up on either side of the front entrance to the house. They welcome in good fortune for the New Year.

Joya no Kane (Ringing the Temple Bell on New Year's Eve)

The ringing of the temple bells marks the coming of the New Year. The bells are rung 108 times during the hour leading up to midnight. In Buddhism, it is said that there are 108 causes of suffering in the world, so for every toll of the bell, one is driven away.

Let's Look More Closely!

We learned a lot about different monthly activities that took place in Japan. Let's go back to look at the main artwork for each month. Remembering what you've learned, look more closely at what the cats and kittens are doing.

January
Looking at all of the kittens, what games and toys can you find them playing with?
Which one would you most like to try?

February
Almost everyone is taking a nap. Which kitten seems to have fallen asleep doing its math homework?
How can you tell it was doing math?

March
Is everyone at the dinner table using chopsticks to eat?
Who's not, and why not?

April
Two of the kittens are returning home from school.
Which two are they? How can you tell?

May
Which cats and kittens are doing something with bamboo?

June
The adults are all carrying things on their backs. Who has come from the fields, and who has come from shopping in town?
How can you tell?

July
Lots of kittens are having fun in this picture. But some are taking naps. How many cats and kittens are taking naps?
Which kitten is playing a trick on two other kittens?

August
Which kittens are listening to a scary ghost story?
Which ones have caught a noisy cicada?

September
How many kittens are hiding among the flowers?
How many dragonflies can you find?

October
Chestnuts have spiky outer shells. Fresh persimmons are sometimes bitter. Rice balls are the perfect picnic food. Can you find kittens with each of these?

November
Leaves are falling off the trees, but other creatures are in them.
How many can you count?

December
Everyone is busy—either cleaning, preparing food, or setting up the New Year's decorations. Can you find the different teams doing each?
Is everyone doing one of these things, or can you find kittens doing something else?

Acknowledgements

We would like to express our special gratitude to the publisher, Eric Oey, for his keen interest and kind support for the book. We would like to extend our heartfelt thanks to the people who have made the book possible, especially our editor, Bob Graham, for his great knowledge and understanding of Japan and for being so nice and enjoyable to work with. Also our warmest thanks go to Genna Manaog, the project manager, and Alphone Tea, the designer. Setsu would also like to thank Richard for his constant support and encouragement. She would also like to express her heartfelt appreciation to Willamarie for her wonderful writing and insight. Willamarie thanks Setsu for her delightful artwork that made writing for this book so much fun!